Susan Hawthorne is a poet, aerialist, publisher and academic. She is the author and editor of numerous books and has contributed to magazines, journals and anthologies in many countries. She is a Research Associate at Victoria University, Melbourne, where she has worked with students who are completing PhDs in creative writing. She is co-founder of Spinifex Press. Her poetry titles include *Bird* (1999), *The Butterfly Effect* (2005), and a co-authored chapbook with Suzanne Bellamy, *Unsettling the Land* (2008). She is also known for performance poetry which combines aerials and text.

Other books by Susan Hawthorne:

Poetry
Unsettling the Land (with Suzanne Bellamy, 2008)
The Butterfly Effect (2005)
Bird (1999)
The Language in my Tongue. In *Four New Poets* (1993)

Fiction
The Falling Woman (1992)

Non-Fiction
Wild Politics (2002)
The Spinifex Quiz Book (1993)

Anthologies
HorseDreams (co-edited with Jan Fook and Renate Klein, 2004)
Cat Tales (co-edited with Jan Fook and Renate Klein, 2003)
September 11, 2001: Feminist Perspectives (co-edited with
    Bronwyn Winter, 2002)
CyberFeminism (co-edited with Renate Klein, 1999)
Car Maintenance, Explosives and Love and other lesbian writings
    (co-edited with Cathie Dunsford and Susan Sayer, 1997)
Australia for Women (co-edited with Renate Klein, 1994)
Angels of Power (co-edited with Renate Klein, 1991)
The Exploding Frangipani (co-edited with Cathie Dunsford,
    1990)
Moments of Desire (co-edited with Jenny Pausacker, 1989)
Difference (1985)

Earth's Breath

SUSAN HAWTHORNE

Where was earth's breath, and blood, and soul?
(Rg Veda 1. 164. 6c)

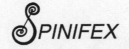

First published in Australia in 2009 by
SPINIFEX PRESS PTY LTD
504 Queensberry Street
North Melbourne, Victoria 3051
Australia
women@spinifexpress.com.au
www.spinifexpress.com.au

Cover design by Deb Snibson, MAPG
Typeset by Claire Warren in Sabon and Zapfino
Printed by McPherson's Printing Group

National Library of Australia Cataloguing-in-Publication entry
Hawthorne, Susan, 1951– .
Earth's breath / Susan Hawthorne.
ISBN 9781876756734 (pbk)
A821.3

for Renate and River
and for all who have been through
breathless calm and wind's rasp

Contents

Prologue: South Mission, 1918

Breathless Calm

Earth's Breath

Wind's Rasp

Prologue: South Mission, 1918

1.
The cyclone is in me as it must have been
in the minds of the Djirrabal people
torn first from land and families
torn from the web of stories
that might have saved them more
than any missionary from foreign lands.

Beachcomber Banfield writes
that it was Old Billy's *milgar*
bark and root entwined
that called up storms of retribution
to his son's competing loves—
two women—
another story of man's fall from grace.

When all the ingredients are right, the cyclone will come—

the ancestors playing their music on the wind
a man stirring his stick in a waterhole
a woman singing to the wind
a drop in air pressure making a wind-swirl roar—
it all amounts to the same thing.

The flightless cassowary bunkers down, feather-wrapped
while other birds gather to fly ahead of the storm
heading inland before the whispering winds
turn to gales—

history repeats itself
the nature of a cyclone is to circle
to turn in on itself
like the ourobouros swallowing its tail
the winged serpent
the snake handing over the apple of unrefined knowledge
to Eve or Lilith or other local heroines—

the end in the beginning
the crossing over of time
as a matrix—
destruction   creation
an endless dance with grinning ghostwinds.

2.
March 10, 1918, beachcomber Banfield
listening to the prattling sea
on the shores of Dunk Island
felt the breathless calm
that precedes every storm.

Within the hours of a day
he was Caliban
on a tempestuous island
where the elements shriek and wail
bodies are flung dead
and half-dead onto the beach.

In the sea were dark patches
scalps of mermaids
wrenched hair of the recently alive.
A great perturbation of wind and flood
that recurs and recurs

These are the forecasts
greenhouse storms
seas no longer prattling
winds becoming great tempests
of the mythic world.

The wind inhales its breathless cloud
the sea exhales coral sand and turtle death
the moon pulls tides
throws up flotsam weed and shell
seas will rise so far
not wave by solitary wave
but by stealth.

The sirens wail for them.
All night long.
How long the night when all the trees are wailing.

Breathless Calm

During a breathless calm a mysterious northerly swell set in. To ears accustomed to the silence and the musical whisperings of a sheltered bay, the roar and burst of the breakers of a wind-forgotten sea suggested a confused mental picture—a blending of black and grey without form.

—E. J. Banfield, *Last Leaves of Dunk*

Timescale

Take a trip to the tropics:
    lie on the beach, snorkel the reef, walk the rainforest
    it can all be done in just a few days—
    you see and you think you see
    but only time brings other ways of seeing

Take a month in the tropics:
    a month when rain falls every day
    ground squelches, mould grows on clothes
    paper wilts with damp and the sky stirs wind

Take a year in the tropics:
    watch the seasons swell—
    the dry crackles and the rainforest opens up
    sunbirds build their nests in doorways
    lizards crunch the undergrowth

Take twenty years:
    you are sure to see a cyclone or two—
    you learn the signs fast, butterfly hordes and stillness
    roaring rain and heaping seas where white foam tumbles

Take today:
    a perfect day in front of a mirror sea—
    looks can deceive
    just wait and see.

Frigatebirds
Fregata minor

The first rainstorm
of the wet season—
two umbrellas folding
and unfolding
plunging seaward

frigatebirds in an
aerial pas de deux
skimming sideways
smooth as the glide
of a French waiter
skipping over

and beneath one another
like thrown stones
on a silent sea.
Today the sea is
roiling, waves breaking

over invisible rocks.
The rain gauge is
overfilled and rising
meanwhile the rumpled
umbrellas unfurl and rise again.

Ourobouros
Liasis olivaceus

The olive python beside the drive
is in a digestive state
having swallowed the world
swallowed the wallaby
body coiled between
branches, almost invisible.

Bicton Hill

Consider the geometry of the spiral
Fibonacci Pythagoras Archimedes
a nautilus shell a sunflower
the curl of a cyclone

walk the spiral path
to the top of Bicton Hill—
walk recursively

in parallel
the sea eagle rises hillside
through the thermals

its way faster and smoother—
the walking path is open
and shaded, rough and flat

white cockatoos screech their
flight over the tree tops
a flight of squawked delight

small seed pods, bright
coloured leaves—red
yellow, green—dot the way

step around the mound
left by the cassowary, the red
fruits of palms digested

this forest has survived more
cyclones than any human
will endure, its tall trees

grounded by vines and
keeled buttressed roots
so many lives at each storey—

canopy, trunk, root—the earth
beside it hosting those ancient
cycad palms grown tall with time

circle the hill looking
out over tropical beaches
island resorts, farms and forests

the finger of the Clump
points seaward, lies low
on the sea, shelters the curl

of Boat Bay where dugong
graze and developers dredge
plans for a pointless marina

this hill with its layers of life
—fruit, flowers, insects, birds—
will go on being what it is

buzzing life inside its own zone
the hill a cone of activity
a monument of solidity

Goodijalla
Haliaeetus leucogaster

Looking up from your desk, you see *goodijalla*
soaring to the sound of a Russian concerto
heavy keyboard with grand sweeps of sound
accompanying long slow eagle wing beat

You dream of freewheeling
threading air through wingtips

Goodijalla, at home over sea, cliffs, rainforest
each afternoon two great eagles fly along
the ridge where the house sits
heaving wings through air, restless as the waves—

in storm, air carries its own weight
on days of sunshine
calm as a whisper
it is light like the blue
of a child's nursery

You move out onto the deck
sit watching the weight of air change.

Sunbird
Nectarinia jugularis

Sunbirds juggle air, zoom the light breezes
spring on fencewires and twigs.

Six thrill seekers
swift as a storm front
dart into heliconia panicles
hang from the lobster petal
sundipping, sucking nightdew
bouncing back to flight.

In the crossroads of the house
a sunbird is building her nest.

She carries in all the hardware
leaf, feather, vine, twig, seedheads
bark strips, one looped
another layered, a helix of debris
turned architectural.

Adding to the string, building on
building out, building down
then—
a leaf and twig porch
that latest extension, feathers inside
cushioning for the tiny life to come.

Anthem to the green tree frog
Litoria infrafrenata

Your croak wakes me from deathlike sleep
just as the seasons pause to reincarnate.
3 am and the world hinge is swinging: opening
closing, the live and the dead are parting.

You wake the dead croaking through the layers
of evolution from your spot next to the screendoor.
The *Mandukya* is in my ears, the brahmins
and the frogs chanting their circular breathing.

Daily I wonder at the painted glee of your
colour, green so green it would make the Irish
envious—I find you sitting in camouflage
on the edge of a leaf or, as tonight, belly-flat

against the glass door waiting for insects—
I've found you visible as daylight, as still
as the soughing night air atop the iron railings.
You play tricks on tourists hiding inside the flange

of the toilet bowl so forever after they'll see
those tiny flat-ended hands grasping—
it's humour and the joy of colour—and of
course the transforming midnight croak.

Year's door

ear to light / standing at the year's door
an insect fluttering inside / a frog at the year's opening
in that tiny space / the space between
lacuna for sound / the scream of a tree frog

amphibious life / the gap the *metaxu*
in two worlds / Janus and Ganesha
door gods / inside outside together
dark with / light at its edge

ear insect fluttering / door frog screaming
batwings in a cave / trapped scream
one wing inside / one leg on the other side
of the dark / body perched in the gap

flight to light / leap to dark
beating wings / bounding legs
panic in my head / terror in its voice
an echo / in the stillness

Sealife

Butterflyfish and seamoth float as you turn
fullcircle undersea. The sea is lucent green
the day you become a fish.

The ocean is the first and last frontier when storms approach
as sea scales grow to wavelets, from horse-crested waves
to turbo white foam, froth and spray.

Dugong shelter in bays like rocks among the seagrass
coral lies exposed at the reef's edge
as vulnerable as damselfish with sweetlips.

Night noises

A long time ago, some god went troppo
in a frenzy of design working up
the rhinoceros beetle. Slam, bash, crack—
it's the sound of failed aerodynamics.

A loud hiss. That same rhinoceros
beetle on its back, legs kicking helpless
to roll or crawl, belly up, feelers flailing
screaming for the hand of god.

The exoskeleton hard as plastic
shiny as ebony but not the brightest
beetle on the block. You pick him up
examine that horn adorning his head

marvel at its baroque excess. You crawl
into bed to the chatter of a family of geckos.
The ones on the white wall are as pale
as plaster. Just as sleep is taking you

a loud thud shocks your eyes open. Dragged
from bed, you stumble out with headlamp torch
to divine the tempest—that tree frog again.
Across the fence bush hens scrabble and squawk.

There *are* silences in the night—as moth
wings sift past your face, as an owl
swoops between branches or a golden
orb spider waits, veiled in intricate architecture.

Storm birds

1. *Scythrops novaehollandiae*

At rest it looks like a boat stranded in a tree
        in flight a crucifix
this bird that holds the record for its size
this surveyor with its angry red eye.

Storm birds, that's what they say
        cuckoos, that's what they are
three of them, black against
the setting sun, crying a throaty song.

Last night the skies opened
this morning it rained yet harder
answering the storm bird's call.

2. *Numenius madagascariensis*

Curlews are calling
presaging wind wail out of stillness.

Silent for weeks
their cry is an agony
the keening wind of dispossessed souls

only stories of the dead unravel
the call of these birds haunting night.

The moon past full
night has emptied a bucket of stars
and the birds still call.

Butterflies
Papilio Ulysses and Ornithoptera priamus

1.

The blue-winged sailor
and the green birdwing
float in on storms—
they like a depression.

A complex of strange
attraction, Psyche
is deserted on a mountain shelf
banished with Zephyr, the west wind.

Coloured dots
rise before the eyes—
like an aura of migraine
or seizure.

The weather
is fitting, cyclonic
not myoclonic;
hectoring.

2.

Butterflies circle
ringing the breezes
orbiting earth from the Amazon
to this Pacific coast.

Windwhirl
music of the spiral spheres
wings in airdrift
butterflies betray the coming storm.

Warning

The warning came four days ahead:
      cyclone heading in—
      but people have lives to live
      and the dinner was not postponed
      the celebration of season's change
      harvest of fruit from tree and vine.

The warning came three days ahead:
      on screen the colours of infrared—
      you talk of the curl on the sea's edge
      aware in a way of what's in store
      you know it's not the same
      for those who've been here before.

The warning came two days ahead:
      the day itself no caveat—
      calculate the weight of wind speed
      all superlatives already stolen
      by cyclone categories one and two
      you cannot weigh any more.

The warning came a day ahead:
      cattle standing in a ring
      rump out, calves surrounded
      wind churn will not move them.

Feast of the senses

The day before the storm
the people of Innisfail
are dancing in
the street, making music

eating tropical fruits—
rambutan yellow and red
mango and mangosteen
crimson dragon fruit and durian

sour sop and Davidson plum
the human taste mimicking
the cassowary—a bird with a
blue bobbing head, a hard

helmet on top, red wattles
and black feathers—the big
bird's kick is as ferocious
as a Category-5 cyclone.

Honey to heliconia

The earth breathes in
holds its breath for a whole day
while we run to prepare
for the exhalation.

A cyclone crouches
flowers bloom
leaf and petal
as if life will go on for ever

a climax of blooming
never so beautiful as today
red green orange pink
against the sea scales

sunbirds have been
following their thrill-
seeking hearts from
honey to heliconia

the horizon is quiet
the air so summer still
no lisp of baby's breath
on our faces

but the web site shows
the huddle beyond sight
tie down the pot plants
in a ribbing of rope

tie the ladder rig the house
pack everything that
moves into the mud room
contemplate the vines

strangling the trees
like the wrenching squeeze
of old Laocöon
we talk over the video

as if it's the last day
of the world and yet
how can we believe it?
you in your flower dress

a camouflage against
the coming wind—
you are weeding:
a lifetime habit

the torch ginger
are growing all on their
own no help from us
butterflies—Ulysses and

birdwing—cavort in the
low pressure rings as the
sun sinks the wind begins
to trek our annihilation

Earth's Breath

They say that a great wind is sweeping the earth.
They say that the sun is about to rise.

—Monique Wittig, *The Guérillères*

Earth's breath

Breath is an origin story
before breath is non-existence
winds ride the edge of the storm
cloud messengers galloping loud
orchestral kettle drums beat.

Summer has been long
its breath has spanned millennia
and now comes the rain
the storm, the raging
rotten breath of cyclonic winds.

Myths are made of such noise
the rampages of Heracles
have filled our childhood ears
the violence of men and gods
he sneezes and we all fall down.

Who will be Delilah, brave enough
to calm Samson with a pair of
scissors, his long hair fallen
trampled like old vines that
strangle the biggest trees?

We are not so lucky with
Larrikin Larry, no shears large
enough to make his pate shine
as we watch, the ground turns bald
with his blunders through the undergrowth.

A shredder over his shoulder, Larry
larks about turning bark and leaves
to confetti and in his next breath
plays graffiti artist, pasting every
wall door and window.

But even wind needs to draw breath
a moment's stillness, earth's smoko—
then we hear the trampling across the roof
the flue knocked off, the guttering
torn ripped and discarded

as Larry changes direction, running rings
widdershins, bellowing earth's grief
no longer at play, this brat is serious
his blood has curdled, our souls are rattled
ears drumming against bawling Larry.

Cyclone time

when earth exhales
we inhale, hold our breath
as that great turbine of wind
rolls over us

three hours we sit
nursing the rising wind
the power goes out
the TV light extinguished

through the window
trees gyrate
wailing to the wind's howl
fascinated in devilish thrall

darkness lopes across the void
of sea in tormented uncertainty
stark-eyed watchfulness
grips us and curiosity listens

6 am we look at one another
gather the bedclothes
move pillows doona
dog into the bathroom

you have the spot by the loo
I have the towel racks
wind thrashes, sky lightens
to grey, the air a roaring

bulldozer in the room
night's stride awash, flecked
with salt I sit in the door jamb
you are videoing

the dawn of a new world
a world of strewn trees
matted leaf torn rooves
metal dress flapping

the dog sleeps on, curled into her
own tight dream 7.30 am
wind turns, limbs snap in fright
lying down for the wind no longer works

light dribbles in, time drags by
I'm reading poetry the space
before me a thinking space
outside a tree branch wings

past the window its leaves
slashing the sky, inside a strange
equilibrium holds me still
in a state of cosmic acceptance

corrugated roof
slams into the garage wall
guttering spills its contents
the down pipe is down

the path spattered confettied
in the pall of wind we poke
our heads into the air
trepidation stalls our steps

Eye of the storm

*All else was dissolved by this lustrous moment made
visible in the eye of the storm.*
    —Patrick White, *The Eye of the Storm*

the eye is not the stillness of fear
the eye patterns the storm

we are the concentric circles of the eye goddess
        the iris of the storm
        the I of the storm

here, the barometric eye
        the panopticon
        the all-seeing eye
        the all-devouring eye

is at the southern edge of the storm
at the immaterial edge of the self

even at the edge of a cliff
ready to take the leap of faith
of love, into the void

here, we are thoroughly material
blown about by the reversing wind

frozen at the edge of nothingness
caught in the torn shreds of leaf matter
    swirled and pasted

the radical, marginalised, left, forgotten
yet the eye, the I, is always central

Into the aftermath

after the violence, the silence—
the wind's roar feels like absence

we tiptoe out as if we
might disturb some giant
asleep in this sepulchre
no bird song

instead a wreckage of foliage
flattened by the wrestler's lock
uprooted bowels of dirt old trunks
snapped triangles

against the new 360 degree view
mountains we've never seen
islands we've tried to
a beach long hidden

I step into a green ants'
nest St Vitus fuelling
my legs into wild dance
the dog refuses this walk

glass in the grass
a mango tree blocks our way
hard to climb over
impossible to go round

we turn back sit on the deck
feeling the sea walling
the garden so close
our verandah coralled

the chimney pot has flown
and the pandanus has been
practising shot put, its fruit
almost at our feet

a solitary pelican floats
in a weeping sky
no power no phone
no water

the clock moves in one time space
our bodies in another, one day by
the clock, years by our bodies
time slicked on our heads

Eyewall

Townships affected by northern and southern portions of the eyewall of the cyclone received the most damage, particularly Babinda and Silkwood ...
Cyclone Larry: Tales of survival from the children of North Queensland

we sit in the space between
      Silkwood and the coast—
the face bricked and mortared
      how much can it see?

the walled eye is half blind
      with fear, the other half
in a state of exhilaration
      dread breaking its own wall—

that eyewall, belting winds
      and menacing rain
we hit the wall, the eyewall—
      staring out across the horizon—

the horizontal centre of our gaze
      in a nearby house a glasswall
explodes glazing splinters across
      the horizon of our view—

How still the world

a spindle seems still
while the threads whirr at the edge
has the world stopped?
have all the humans fallen
off this spinning top?

perhaps it's only us
left to our solitary epiphanies
the fragilities of twigs
and birds, trees and stalks

no Noah couple us
we move around the house
the garden like ants
in a raided nest

through the death silence
from the mountains
comes the welcome scream
of a chainsaw
bouncing off naked trunks

our neighbour appears through
the sticks of a ragged tree
calling as he approaches
his long-limbed frame
like a tree from Dunsinane

pyjama-clad we elaborate
our survival among the
rainforest ruins
against the vastness of the wind

Canticle

The weather is as volatile
as an economy in crisis—

a triangle of hope—
seven frigatebirds flying in formation
days crawl by in silence
and a frenzy of work

we collect fragments of roof
stacked like discarded toys
from a broken Leggo set
I carry a length of guttering

over my shoulder across
a rubble of trees
the broom has never been
used so much in so short

a time I sweep paths
walls doors windows
the underside of the roof
shredded leaf matter fills

my mind my hands
sticks to my bare feet
the heliconia are ground
down tattered and bruised

their dresses a torn swathe
of broken red flowers
the butterflies still wing by
but only two sunbirds return

collecting honey from the
still-flowering collapsed stems
my body is abuzz with
adrenalin the muscles

afright with the energy
of disaster day after day
our hearts beat
in syncopated arhythmia

I climb I walk I carry I sweep
I mop I wash I wipe I weep

the ache in my feet
hollows of motion
we rush to close up
against more wind and rain

waiting without end for
the sun to spill through
with sleep we open the psyche
to a canticle of pain

Helicopter breath

The sun is barely up when the helicopter comes over
its blades whirring like that old wind

inside the chopper someone is winding out the film
(well, the video on some kind of tape made up of digits
not the finger type either)

and you can almost see the shocked looks on their faces
they're so close they must be seeing this destruction

like it's a matchbox disaster, and some kid's come along
in a tantrum kicked the toys all about, stomped on
them, you know

they swarmed in these SES types dressed like wasps in
their orange overalls carrying chainsaws as if they were
machine guns

one bloke gets his chainsaw stuck in the tree then
another and another like it's some kind of stuck-
chainsaw epidemic

then I look round and you're laughing, turning and
laughing so they don't see your face

because you know there's nothing more a man hates
than being laughed at by a woman

and you know that and turn away because they're
carrying chainsaws

and laughing by a woman when a man's got a chainsaw
is like throwing lit dynamite into a drum of petrol
real explosive

by the time the wasps leave you've calmed down a bit
and I see you walk away almost breathless

I was thinking about these big winds and how they
just steamroll you flat as a lizard

afterwards you somehow have to keep on through all
the soreness that comes when you don't sleep properly

all the huffing and puffing from working without a
break from nightmares and chainsaws and early
rising helicopters.

Lifting the roof

the Mourilyan Hotel
is folded like an origami swan—
some houses look
untouched from one side
but around the corner they
turn out to be Evita façades

once a house is pried open
it is prey to the wind
one verandah unfastened
like a can opened—
the roof lifting its lid
flipped and fell back

these are houses of cards
fragile and limp, roofing
bent like a child's toy
traffic lights point to the sky
bananas are mashed with soil
a kitchen sink in the grass

broken bricks are heaped
on the hood of a new car
a hills hoist is hoisted and shattered
tattered metal and wire
a boat listing grounded
the scenic drive sign surreal

at the weighbridge
along the tourist road
the corrugated shed
once flat-sided is cantilevered
like a giant bird hide
with its cold eye on the world

Chaos across the land

The reporter stands among the chaotic trees with the mike
in her hand. She's droning with the buzz of media speak …
silence across the land … like a war zone.

> *Come off it*, I shout at the video
> I couldn't watch in real time

… defoliated trees … powerlines kiss the ground.

> What she's really trying to say is that the trees
> lie in awful abandon, the school is junked.

> Behind her is a straggling group of porous people
> she hasn't noticed and on the soundtrack
> (uncommented upon) are sirens.

> No one ties me to the mast to stop me listening.

The only thing that makes you think war is all those khakied
boys in stranded army trucks who don't know what they're
doing. Military hardware and proliferating personnel.

She's talking again to a man
who says turning towards his house
Where do you start?

On the window sill is a child's teddy drying in the sun
the house is tarped and wrapped like a Christos artwork.

You can see the psychic rebellion in some people's faces
as they tell stories of survival and entrapment

... the roof flew four hundred metres ... hit the house. ...

*The stack on the sugar mill crunched even before
the biggest winds struck. ...*

The baker says *... drove home at 5.30 am the car rocked
with the wind. ... Next door the top half of the house
was shaved off.*

... Larry destroyed everything. ... It was the second wind,
the last one said, *that tore the house apart.*

The camera pans a landscape of skeletons
trees in spiral twist, trunks unbarked, vertebrae exposed
tarsal and metatarsal, twig and branch.

Maruts: storm demons

Afterwards, like new lovers telling stories
we talk of all the storms we've ever
witnessed, all the storms
that have snatched at our lives. Stories make
sense of our new state of existence
in the post-cyclone world.

I tell you how dust storms coloured
my childhood, the blue sky died
to dark, then red with dust.
We ran to every window: bolt shut
pull down the blinds, tie in a
figure-of-eight, our mother calling
out each place, *Is this checked?*
What of that? The doors closed
with dust-jamming snakes.
A cold wind runs over the roof
blasting us, and later we roam the house
drawing stick figures in the dust.

You trump me. Tell me of the
sandstorm in Tunisia, getting caught
out in it, not listening closely enough
to the locals' warnings. Ant-watching
you miss all the signs until it's
almost too late. Diving into
the car, you plug every gap, every millimetre
but still the sand comes in. You say

It's the roar of the wind that is the same.

I remember the snowstorm on
Mt Kosciusko. It is nearly summer and
we leave the resort after lunch
dressed only in shorts and T-shirts, walking
compassless, we follow the snowpoles
losing our place on the map, not really
knowing our course. Unplanned, late
afternoon we stumble on Seaman's Shack
a stone hut above the treeline. In falling
dark, I go in search of firewood
finding a single fallen pole. We cook
eat half-warmed food and pull the
sleeping bags over our heads. At midnight
the roar comes, the wind blizzarding
the walls. We lie with our bodies
curling the stovelegs, our ears filled with
the resounding echo of storm demons.

With each storm story, another
ricochets through our brains, our
startled synapses in overload. The
flood of '74, the fires, the snowstorms
in your home country. You say
it's like being in a washing machine
tumbled, thrown, strewn driftwood.

Slash and burn

We replant trees swirled from their roots
pile earth around a patch of undergrowth
bailed up against the fence
like the victim of a daylight robbery.

Slash and burn
lets in the light, makes forest into life.
Like the mosaic burners
fire renews, breaks open seed pods
here the stomach of the cassowary
breaks it down.

Spin for an hour and whirl
alternately in opposite directions
advised Rudolf Steiner. This cyclone
is the planet's biodynamic gardener.

In this scrap of ground, the wind
spiralled its way through, scattered
the greenery, piled it in heaps—
life imitating art, nature imitating people.

It's hard to know whether gathering
the dead will make or unmake us.

Every leaf turns: where the cyclone
came past, leaves die, yet some
turn again to life. Where the fire
came through, the human wildfire
nothing recovers, burnt to a cinder.

The small burn is different
like the tree outside the cyclone's edge
leaves are ruffled, some fall
even the occasional tree is ready
to fall. Light comes in again.

Body roar

blood on a leaf
gold trace element in water
light from the eye behind the eye
     —Adrienne Rich, *The school among the ruins*

1.
The human body
moans
from its depths
like earth roar
from earth core

this roaring *is* inside her

the body speaks
its unvoiced pain

on the surface
waves rolling
the spinal ridge
erupts

2.
Five bodies
like five digits

of one palm
waving

3.
The tree
has roots

as the tree is
uprooted
it too moans

Fool's Lear

a conference in Durban
takes us out of the zone
but the cyclone still
fibrillates our minds—

in KwaZulu Natal
the king goes nowhere
without his praise singer
like Fool's Lear

today's poet
takes out her chainsaw
shouting poems to the wind

they fall on deaf ears
the birds have stopped singing
even the buzz of insects is stilled

the chainsaw screams
into her fuelless dreams

Frenzied

Three weeks have passed, I've changed countries
my psyche is excess baggage, carrying an
unexpected weight, dreamlife and waking life
crosshatch into fantasy and fearfulness.

The elephant matriarchs walk so lightly on the veld,
kudu do disappearing tricks behind twigs. The night
world is far less friendly. I wake shaken too scared
to close my eyes, the scream strangling my breath.

Choking on the memory of certain death, I know
that this time I have taken one risk too many. The
wind swells in me with its ravages. A walking
catastrophe, I am goaded by furious tempests.

Shattered dreams

on our return to Australia
our neighbour says

*the trees that are dead
are shattered on the inside*

you say, *the people that are quiet
are shattered on the inside*

The cyclone inside

Are we ready for the wind?
... Will this wind come inside us?
—Susan Griffin, *Woman and Nature*

Four months have passed—
the dreams settled
no midnight crying
no calling out for help

We make
a casual visit to the gallery
skipping the meeting like two
schoolgirls playing truant

And then I hear it—

the earth roaring as if death has come
the water rages we are mere twigs
floating, broken by the water's wash
and the wind—

the wind is inside me
I am not ready for this cave-in
on the gallery floor
as the installation rolls on

earth roaring, water roaring
and this— this— cyclone inside

Dancing pair

my dog and I are pissing on the moonlit lawn
rainforest echoes the cry of night birds
cheering the Chinese-lantern moon
the melaleuca has a collar of leaves
rising up its trunk, but they've a long way
to go before shading my eyes from the light

this is one of two dancing trees
the other is bedraggled
leafless and lightless
like the betrayed partner of a dancing pair
the dying tree bisects the moon's beam
its leaves a counterfeit dress

but it's a vaporous veil
and clouds quilt threaded stories
the sea flat in imitation, the moon's
light reflects dully on oceanic tides
like light at the edge of the universe
scalloped clouds embroider the sky

Three saints

on the first Sunday of May
the bells in Silkwood
ring out, a cannon is fired
the procession wends its way
along the muddy path
yesterday our neighbours said

It'll be fine tomorrow
It's the feast of the three saints

and right on cue the sky clears
rain stops, a child holds the
hand of a grandfather
a pregnant woman carries
the next generation

(elderly men in their Sunday best)
a young girl has a frangipani
caught in her hair, a group of girls
are parading in peasant dress
spotted kerchiefs on their heads—

the gold palanquin is
decorated with bougainvillea
red green and blue trimmings
you queue for hot chestnuts
under the marquee

this year so many come
so many whose rooves
have escaped their moorings
so many with houses
doing penance so much
cleaning up still to do—

I hear the *prophetic screams*
of those three youths San Filadelfo
San Alfio and San Cirino
transplanted to the canefields
and lament that it does not
bring balance to the world
nor relief to the heart

Moondark

Half a year after Larry
my life's as flat as the moon's
dark. Is it Larry or some-
thing else? I blame the

rampaging wind for
creating the skeleton
trees. I blame
this giant eye for exposing

all the weaknesses
all the fractures.
I blame a barometric
depression for my mood.

Even the curlews know
as they whistle up
the souls of the dead while
darkness creeps into me.

Strike it down, I read.
Depression *is* down.
Strike it down, lay waste
the land, the body

the fracture in the soul
gaping goggle-eyed at the
dark rim of the horizon
and no moon to mourn.

Forest
Casuarius casuarius johnsonii

no wabu, no wuju, no gunduy
no forest, no food, no cassowary

—Djiru saying.

A girl goes into the forest
the forest is a rainforest
her guide is a cassowary
the cassowary knows her way through the forest
she knows all the fruits of the forest
she is mistress of the forest
the fruits are red blue orange green and yellow
the girl must collect the fruit

Along comes a big wind
a wind that lifts and
twists the trees round and round
so that their trunks are spiralled
the wind hauls trees out of the earth
and throws them every which way
the girl shelters under the heavy black feathers
of the cassowary which pin her to the ground

When the big wind has passed
the girl is disoriented
she no longer knows which way is up
she hardly knows which is east or west
which is sun which is moon

clouds scud across the sky
but they have lost their shapes
no longer are there stories in the clouds
just loss

The cassowary tries to comfort the girl
at first there is plenty of fruit
fallen fruit native plum lilly pilly quandong
the girl wanders behind disconsolately
from time to time she nibbles at the rotting flesh
but it soon sours
the bitter seed takes over from the soft flesh

As the days pass
the cassowary must wander further and further afield
she ventures into places she's never been before
followed by the girl
soon the fruit is nowhere to be found
the two sit down to wait for windfall
quietly they drop into sleep
quietly they die

Cassowary types

You know, there'll be lots of cassowary people there.
Huh, what d'ya mean? Cassowary people? D'ya mean
the sort that have a cast of a cassowary at their front gate?
D'ya mean the sort who collect cassowary toys? Or d'ya
mean those greenie types, you know the sort that harp on
and on about how special them big birds are? I mean,
ya know they're not bad these birds. Didja know that
it's the boys who bring up the chicks in the cassowary
family? I reckon that's how it oughta be. They been
hangin round these parts for nigh on three million
years. Ya know, that's stayin power, mate. I reckon
they're pretty good lookin too, that nice mix of blue
and red against them black feathers. 'd make a nice
hat those feathers. Ooh shouldn I've said that about
the hat, sorry kid. *D'ya want to come to the exhibition
then? See some photos of those good lookin birds? Come
on, why not?* Well. Okay then. But only if ya tell me
the story again about how the cassowary kicked its
way through a Category-5 cyclone and survived. I know
the poor things were starving after Larry and all those
posh groups with promotion in their names did bloody
nothin about it. Well, I reckon this art stuff is probably
okay. Can ya give me a lift to the openin then?

Ark

They gather us two by two
the men and women in polished green
who pray to Saint Larry
the razer, the clearer
the saviour who needs pay
no tithe to the people.

They are parrots
repeating the mantra—

information sharing
information sharing.

The Ark is engrossed
in capital-K Knowledge—
our knowledge—
where do they live—
what tracks do they follow—
what fruits do they eat?

They are pirates and the locals
are hooked.
Well-practised ignorance
how much is innocence—
as each living thing marches
to the tune of old Noah—

Ham is there to help
but Mrs Noah has other
things to do, she has
volunteered her services—

to the rescue Mrs Noah

The Ark cares for the
future—they say so in all
their documents, repeat
it as often as possible—
we've all heard them.

The crew on the Ark
remain behind doors
seated at red cedar
desks, polished to reflect
them at twice their size.

The skipper and first
mate take the blows—
They lower the gangplank
and count the animals
the birds, the frogs
the insects, the humans—
even the trees move.

The gangplank is raised—
All mine, says Noah
peering between
the bars of his invisible cage—
a cage without walls
he protests.

You say, *It's like*
a war without casualties.

Candlesticks

Two years on and the forest
surrenders, holds up
its empty-handed
petrified limbs. Birds
come and go, visible
now on the wind-
stripped boughs.

The dead tree tops
are candelabra
against the sunset
twig and stick flaring
into light.

The spangled
drongo swoops in
shadow black, alighting
on the flagellated
trunks, calling down the dark
chattering silence.

Wind's Rasp

Moths rushing full tilt to their ruin
fly right into an inferno
                    —Bhagavad Gita 11.29

Wind's rasp

1.
The wind never splinters at the edge
never

yesterday and the days before
were perfect
still
as the butterflies
zoned in on the depression

on this day
a dying bird
with no call left
shattered by the wind's antics

2.
How does a pelican know
when it's safe to fly in
fly over in solitary silence
bringing hope?

Can seven frigatebirds
calculate a week, a day each?

Can infinity be eclipsed
or pain recalculated by the
Vedic mathematician?

3.
How will the winds
tell us the future?

It's thirty years since the orang utan
in the zoo
beneath the sun's eclipse
stood tom-tomming his chest
on the broken tree angled skyward

on the other side of the wall
the cats mewl for early dinner
and the streets go quiet
while the people watch
the darkening skies on television
with two few lines for resolution

4.
The dark hurlings of nature
are terror enough for our reptile brains.
When man-made horrors occur
will the albatross fly in
to watch the carnage?

I don't recall birds
on the day the towers fell

but here on the beach
after the wind's ripping
rasp
are ten black cockatoos
calmly eating the spilt seed

5.
This woman—
descended from bird, primate and cat—
stance aslant, her eyes levelled at yours
can she see the horizon?

Yugantameghaha

At the end of every cosmic cycle
at the end of a generation—*yuganta-*
meghaha—clouds congregate
gathering souls for the next *yuga*

cloud breath, soul mist
rasping winds, rattling bones
here come the galloping horses
humans astride their flanks

here come the thundering clouds
breaking the world apart
the Hercules moth climbs every building
rising upwards through 110 floors

scaling the earth to find the moon
that light in the sky through which
he might escape earth's pull
and melt into the inferno of light.

Sista Katrina
Katrina, New Orleans, USA, 29 August 2005

The wind came back with triple fury, and put out the light for the last time. They sat in company with the others in other shanties, their eyes straining against crude walls and their souls asking if He meant to measure their puny might against His. They seemed to be staring at the dark, but their eyes were watching God.
—Zora Neale Hurston, *Their Eyes Were Watching God*

Out of the night come the words of Zora Neale Hurston
who must have sat out her own Sister Katrina or Brother
Larry in the Everglades more than half a century ago.

Her words gather up the lives of the Seminoles, the people
of the Glades who vacated the hurricane zone days ahead of
everyone else. What is it that they know?

When Katrina came knocking what they had known was all
long forgotten. In Pearlington, *Cookie had ridden out
seven storms before Katrina*, but she says she ain't
     staying for the eighth.

She has seen the casino that swam across the highway
the boats grounded between the fountain and the garden
plots the steps leading nowhere, a place scoured of hope.

The tidal surge deluged towns with Biblical force, the local
church an ark without Noah at its helm. Instead of prayers
mobile phone numbers are emblazoned on still-standing walls.

In the next township a house of unstacked walls vies
with an uncovered slab for space in the world's newspaper
pages. The tales not heard are the days of waiting.

Days when you look at the poles of your home, wondering
where the walls went. Days of scrubbing and cleaning a task
that seems as endless as the ocean now beating at your door.

There are days of boredom, when it gets too much when
you want your old mattress, now sodden among the rubbish.
It changes you for ever.

Bhumiheen
Sidr, Bangladesh, 15 November 2007

When a cyclone hits the coast
of Bangladesh, the world's media
hardly murmurs. In their minds
Bangladesh is basketcase.

Post-cyclone, few have
a roof over their head, the well-off
are in houses built of scraps of tin
smoothed mud floors.

The latrine pot has floated away
the cooking pots too. Branches
of broken trees are the flimsy
foundation for the next house.

Says one, We are *bhumiheen*
bhumi—land, *heen*—less.
And, he adds, *heen* in everything.
A woman has lost her cows

lost her wealth. I read about Sidr
not in a glossy hardbound book
but on paper printouts of Rokeya's
email. I am struck by the pain

in New Orleans and Bangladesh
alike, but no one knows the name
of the cyclone in Bangladesh
only the numbers.

Irrawaddy speechless
Nargis, Burma, 7 May 2008

1.
The wind is roaring from the TV screen—
the same wind rasping through me.

Each time the wind scrapes people from
the earth's surface I am in it all over again.
I cry with the woman whose face is stained
with tears, ramshackle walls behind her.

The wind still roaring inside her—
television news unravelling me.

The coastline changes shape, her country
impenetrable and still the generals do nothing.
Five days since the wind pounced like a Bengal tiger
waves pouring through the houses washing away all.

2.
The mouths of the Irrawaddy have been silenced
in a gurgle of seawater, the Irrawaddy
is garrotted, throttled
the voices of the people strangled.

How can we ever know how many have died—
no one knows how many have lived.

The mouths of the Irrawaddy are no longer restive
stitched into silence these lips can hardly breathe
The mouths of the Irrawaddy spill breathless words
crying out against the bruising of the land.

Hide and seek
Charlotte, Australia, 12 January 2009

Charlotte's winds rise early on the wing, heliconia
throb a frantic dance at the deck's edge and the Torres
Strait pigeons errand by like a group of teenage girls.

At daybreak we are climbing the hill against the wind
and the coming rain; descending, the world has
changed, waterfalls sprout from the hillside.

Sunbird fledglings left the nest three days ago in
anticipation of local flooding, of the need to get those
wings airborne before winds knocked them sideways.

The sea swallows sand on the beach, carving a new
geography, river edged, sand gouged, water vomited
from the usually placid pools that amble shoreward.

The summer's wet is full of surprises, cane toads are
showering in daylight, the tiny cassowary chick is
taking a walk up the road's red embankment.

The bridge to the main road is flooded, drowning gravel
even the sign showing its depth is sunk; like sprouting
waterfalls the creek falls back as fast as it came.

Ellie, Australia, 1 February 2009

There is something about the light
the day before the winds come—
emerald grass against sapphire hills
the colour stark and clear, outlined.

Later flying through cloud I am
struck by the fibrous strands of
water droplets. Behind these wisps of
intangibility lies a cyclone.

Hamish, Australia, 8 March 2009

The silver hammer of Hamish is held high
threatening to land on someone's head
but Hamish is more elusive than most
keeping his hands off the coast, staying

well away from land. He's playing with us
turning in fast circles like a kilted hammer
thrower, the chained ball flying wide catching
the watchers at the edge unawares.

Wind mind

1.
Sitting on the edge of my chair
waiting to hear
waiting to hear
if the winds have come again

Standing in the supermarket
feeling the roar
feeling the roar
as if the winds have come again

Lying on the grass
watching the clouds
watching the clouds
knowing the winds have come again

2.
Think of the breath of a cyclone:
breathing warm ocean surface air
exhausting the cold air above
driving up its intensity

Sea-churning super typhoon
Fengshen strikes the Philippines
in the Caribbean Fay, Gustav, Hannah and Ike:
sea heat / hurricane wind

3.
What we know:
we who live in houses
with walls and windows
strong enough to withstand the wind

Fraudulent is how I feel
sympathy in my gut
but I am one of hundreds
whose house still stands

The wind has entered
some inner part of me
and I cannot wrench it out
but I am not drowning in the scouring sea

4.
she dreams of going to a place where there is no air
pressure no up and no down a world of blue with
flashes of colour and a firm rock to hide under she
dreams of moving three hundred and sixty degrees
without her feet solid on sand she floats belly down
among the seaweed and the big spotted cod then

rolls over and watches the light falling through the
water like diamond rain but instead her lungs are
filled with fuming vapours and the air presses hard
on her jamming her between earth and sky she runs
head first into the tree trunk clasps its hard skin to
her skin she scratches her hands on sharp twigs and falls

5.
I am in with through the cyclone
which is inside with through me
the cyclone which is at the heart of things
the cyclone which is at the edge of chaos
we too are like the swirling objects
in a Remedios Varo painting
twirling spiralling simultaneously
at the edge and at the centre of the
universe in a massive creation of life
we are the cross-hatched winds of
Gungara the spiralling wind
from the Kimberleys, we are a poet
defiantly writing herself into creation
and as I rise from bed to write
I see that the dog has a paw
across your shoulder and it seems to
epitomise what I am struggling to express

Notes

p. iii, *Rg Veda* 1. 164. 6c
This citation from the *Rg Veda* comes from Wendy Doniger O'Flaherty. 1980. *Women, Androgynes, and Other Mythical Beasts.* Chicago: University of Chicago Press. p. 19.

p. ix, Mission Beach lies in the zone of tropical cyclones. Its history is pocked by cyclones and storms, some with devastating effects. Home originally to the Djirbalngan-speaking people—now known as Djiru —in the 19th century they saw explorers and prospectors, foresters, farmers and fishers enter their country. The Cutten Brothers moved in permanently in 1882, clearing the land of red cedar and silky oak, growing bananas, pineapples, coconuts as well as tea and coffee. Chinese farmers grew bananas along the Tully River, employing the local Aboriginal people, but opium addiction became rife. On the Hull River, a settlement was built, ostensibly to counter the problems of conflict and addiction. But it had other purposes. From across Queensland, Aboriginal people were brought to this settlement in chains. The locals euphemistically called it "the mission". In 1918, a great cyclone swept away Indigenous and coloniser alike and although "the mission" was not rebuilt, the name remained. Post-cyclone, many of the Indigenous people were displaced and forcibly moved to Palm Island.

p. ix, Edmund James Banfield (1852–1923) was the son of a printer and newspaperman who migrated from Liverpool to the Victorian goldfields in 1854. As a young man, Banfield moved north and took up a post as journalist and sub-editor on the *Townsville Bulletin* when miners were its main readership. Banfield spent twenty-five years living on Dunk Island which lies just off the coast from Mission Beach. He wrote extensively about the environment and the history of the local Aboriginal people. He was on Dunk Island when it was struck by what appears to have been a Category-4 or -5 cyclone on 10 March 1918.

p. x, "prattling sea": "the sea will prattle to him" E. J. Banfield. *The Gentle Art of Beachcombing*, edited by Michael Noonan. St Lucia: UQP, 1989. p. 155.

p. xi, "scalps of mermaids": E. J. Banfield. 1925. *Last Leaves of Dunk*. A Project Gutenberg of Australia eBook. p. 5.

p. 1, "breathless calm": E. J. Banfield. 1925. *Last Leaves of Dunk*. p. 1.

p. 7, goodijalla is the Djiru word for sea eagle.

p. 9, The Mandukya is part of the cycle of Upanishads written in Sanskrit. In the *Mandukya Upanishad* the croaking of the monsoonal frogs is compared to the chanting of the Brahmins. Mandukya means frog.

p. 17, The annual harvest festival in Innisfail held to coincide with the equinox.

p. 18, the web site: Bureau of Meteorology, http://www.bom.gov.au/

p. 21, Monique Wittig. 1970. *The Guérillères*. London: Picador. p. 70.

p. 22, Tropical Cyclone Larry developed off the eastern Australian coast over the Coral Sea on 16 March. By Friday, it was headed straight for us at Bingil Bay. It crossed the coast of Queensland at Latitude 17 degrees South on the morning of Monday 20 March 2006. The eye of the storm was centred on the town of Innisfail. Three of us, two women and a dog, were located on the edge of the cyclone where winds are strongest. Larry proceeded to travel inland, affecting those on the Atherton Tableland. In the hours before its arrival we watched on computers and TV the cyclone's track towards us across the ocean. Satellite images create beautiful swirling colours that resemble a bright galaxy. There is some debate about the wind strength. In Innisfail, it was Category-4. At the edges, at the eyewall, it was probably a Category-5. The tipping point between Category-4 and -5 is whether winds are at speeds of less or more than 280 km per hour.

p. 27, Patrick White. 1980. *The Eye of the Storm*, London: Penguin. p. 410.

p. 31, *Cyclone Larry: Tales of survival from the children of North Queensland*. 2006. Innisfail: Mothers Helping Others Inc.

p. 36, SES: State Emergency Service, a voluntary service for mutual assistance in times of disaster.

p. 40, Some images and quotations in this poem are drawn from a documentary DVD. Frank Russo. 2006. *The Eye of Larry*. A Digital Memories Production.

p. 42, Maruts are Indian storm gods or demons who exemplify different aspects of wind. The Maruts run wild alongside the powerful figure of Indra who is associated with the monsoons.

p. 46, Adrienne Rich. 2004. *The school among the ruins*. New York: Norton & Norton. p. 81.

p. 48, Soon after the cyclone, a conference in Durban takes us out of the country. In Durban, the King of KwaZulu Natal opens the conference. Leading the king is a quiet dignified man, the ceremonial Praise Singer.

p. 51, Susan Griffin. 1978. *Woman and Nature: The roaring inside her*. Harper & Row: San Francisco. p. 22.

p. 53, Silkwood, one of the hardest hit towns, has an annual festival on the first Sunday in May. This festival originates in Sicily and was brought to Silkwood by Rosario Tornabene in thanks for the survival of his wife and daughter following a life-threatening childbirth. The festival attracts the many descendants of Italian immigrants from across north Queensland.

p. 54, "Prophetic screams": Walt Whitman. 1986. *Leaves of Grass*. New York: Penguin Books. p. 51.

p. 56, The cassowary is a flightless bird that has wandered the rainforest for millions of years and has adapted quite well to exotic fruits like mango, apple and banana. After a cyclone it broadens its diet. But it is more difficult for it to adapt to cars and deforestation. Its health is tied to the health of the rainforest, and the rainforest depends on the cassowary to eat fruit in order to germinate the seeds. Following Cyclone Larry many cassowaries died of starvation.

p. 63, *Bhagavad Gita* 11.29. Translation, Susan Hawthorne.

p. 67, Yugantameghah is a Sanskrit word meaning a gathering of clouds at the end of an epoch; a yuga is an epoch and some say we are currently living in the Kali yuga, an epoch of destruction.

p. 68, Zora Neale Hurston. 1979. *Their Eyes Were Watching God*. Urbana: University of Illinois Press. p. 236.

p. 68, Sally Pfister and Melody Golding. 2007. *Katrina: Mississippi Women Remember*. University Press of Mississippi. pp. 16–20.

p. 70, In November 1991, 100,000 people died following a cyclone and tidal surge. For many, this is the prevailing image of Bangladesh, so when Cyclone Sidr hit in 2007, the media reported it for just a few days. Bhumi is the Bengali word for land; bhumi-heen means land-less.

Acknowledgements

Poems in this collection have been previously published (some in different forms) in *The Age*, *Westerly*, *Ripple Project*, *Five Bells*, *Queensland Arts*, *PEN Newsletter*, *Mission Beach Bulletin* (Australia), *Sinister Wisdom* (USA), *Best Australian Poems 2008*, edited by Peter Rose, and *Paradise Anthology*, edited by Michael Crane.

Thank you to all involved in the publishing of this book, to the women at Spinifex Press: Nikki Anderson, Maralann Damiano, Jo O'Brien and Camille Nurka who have made the publishing of this collection a delight; to designer Deb Snibson and typesetter Claire Warren for their visual acumen.

Enormous thanks to my readers, without whom this book would wear its flaws more openly. To Robyn Edwards, Patricia Sykes, Gina Mercer and Robyn Rowland who gave the manuscript detailed poetic attention. Their comments and critiques opened the work to new ideas, and I thank them all for their seriousness of reading. Heartfelt thanks to Patricia Sykes for her careful editing, her radical suggestions and enjoyable conversation. To my partner Renate Klein who not only read with her usual sharp intelligence but has been with these poems since their first breath a few days after Cyclone Larry hit in March 2006. Together we sat through the turbo-charged winds and the snap of psychic recoil in the aftermath. Our much-loved dog, River, was there too, doing the usual emotional housework that dogs are so good at, while her successor, Freya has made me take numerous walks during the rewriting and editing.